Journey to Jericho

Joshua lived a long time ago. His [...] exciting story. Have you heard of Mos[es ...] character from the Bible? Well, Mo[ses ...] people of Israel, God's special people, out of Egypt. They were going to live in a new place... The Promised Land. There they expected things to be wonderful. For the moment they are travelling round the Wilderness being fed on manna and quail provided by God. We join them as Moses receives a special message from God about the way they have to live.

God told Moses that he wanted to speak to him and so he had to go to the top of Mount Sinai. God wanted to make sure that the people lived at peace with each other and did not harm each other. For this to happen God wanted them to have some rules.

What sort of things do you do that you need rules for? Unjumble the following words to find out:

AMGSE _ _ _ _ _   **FILE** _ _ _ _   **RTFFICA** _ _ _ _ _ _ _

OOBLLAFT _ _ _ _ _ _ _ _   **CHSLOO** _ _ _ _ _ _

Look at the pictures below. In which picture are the people obeying the rules?

What would happen to traffic on the road if there were no rules of the road?

_____

These special rules are called the Ten Commandments. Can you match the stones together to make up the ten pairs of stones. Watch out you might find this a bit tricky! The answers are at the back of the book if you get stuck. If you find some of these commands difficult to understand then look up page 31.

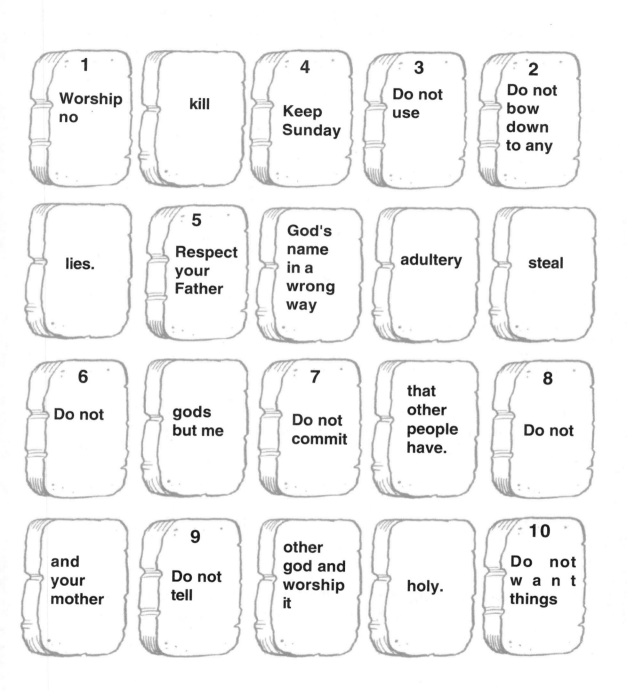

1 Worship no

kill

4 Keep Sunday

3 Do not use

2 Do not bow down to any

lies.

5 Respect your Father

God's name in a wrong way

adultery

steal

6 Do not

gods but me

7 Do not commit

that other people have.

8 Do not

and your mother

9 Do not tell

other god and worship it

holy.

10 Do not want things

Moses had to write this message out on big pieces of stone. He had been up on the mountain with Joshua his helper but only Moses had been close to God. He was up there for forty days and forty nights.

Sadly while he was away the people became bored and told Aaron so. (Aaron was Moses' brother). They began to think that Moses wasn't going to come back. They all decided to do a really bad thing. They made a god for themselves. They brought all their gold, melted it down and carved it into the shape of a calf. The next day they bowed down to worship this god. God was very angry.

Join the dots to see the calf they made.

When Moses saw what was going on when he returned he broke the special pieces of stone and burned the calf. Draw flames around the calf to show it burning.

More trouble came on the people but eventually God let Moses write out the commands again. As the Israelites got close to the land of Canaan God told Moses to send some men ahead to see what the land was like. However, they came back with different reports. Unjumble the words to find out what they thought of the land.

ti ahs oodg doof

__ ___ ____ ____

ew nac fteade htem

__ ___ _____ ____

erthe rea guhe ctiies

_____ ___ ____ _____

eyth vaeh rtogsn llaws

____ ____ _____ _____

teh eoplep rea gib nda trosng

___ _____ ___ ___ ___ _____

The Israelites forgot to trust God and were too scared to enter Canaan. As punishment they had to wander in the desert for 40 years. Joshua and Caleb were the only two people who trusted God. Moses became old and God told him that Joshua was to lead the people. With God's help Joshua was to take the people over to the new land. Moses would see the land in the distance but he would not go there himself. There was a big task ahead of Joshua as he had to lead the people forward.

God gave Joshua a promise to help him. All the vowels have been missed out. See if you can put them in to find out what the promise was.

Vowels: a, e, i, o, u.

__s __ w__s w__th M__s__s s__

w__ll __ b__ w__th y__ __.

God also told him

B__ str__ng __nd

c__ __r__g__ __ __s

__nd __b__y my l__w.

God still wants us to obey him today and follow his law.

```
┌ ─ ─ ─ ─ ─ ─ ─ ─ ─ ─ ─ ─ ┐
│ FACT: Laws were kept in │
│ the ark of the covenant. │
└ ─ ─ ─ ─ ─ ─ ─ ─ ─ ─ ─ ─ ┘
```

Everyone started to get ready to go into the promised land, they had all been looking forward to this for so long. Joshua sent his men around the camp telling everyone that in three days they would move forward into the land God had promised to them. Can you draw in the route the people have taken since leaving Egypt?

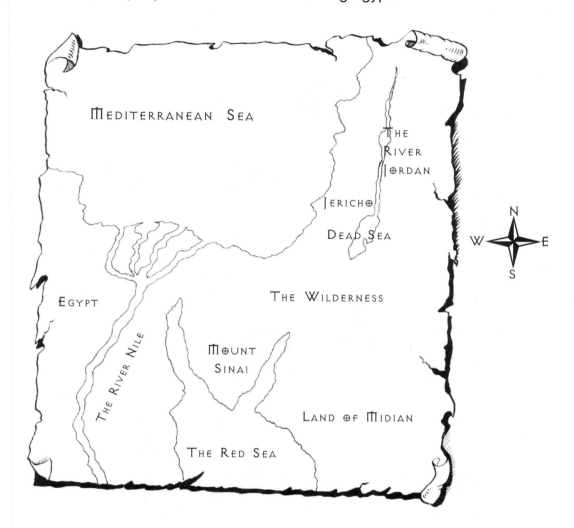

Start at Egypt and go south over the Red Sea to Mount Sinai then head north to the Wilderness, zig-zag around the Wilderness because they lived and travelled around there for forty years, head east out of the wilderness and then turn north and come into Jericho. Mark in some pyramids at Egypt, some mountains around Sinai and some walls at Jericho. Colour it in too.

7

Without anyone knowing about it, Joshua sent two spies over into the land to see what it was like. They were told to especially see what the city of Jericho was like. They went to the city and went to the house of a lady called Rahab. While they were there the king heard about their arrival and he sent a message to Rahab. Find the words hidden in the picture and unjumble them to see what the message was.

__ __ __ __ ___ ___ ___ ___ ___

____ __ ___. ____ ___ __

__ __ __ __ __.

But Rahab had hidden them on her roof under some stalks of flax. She told the spies that she had heard all that God had done and how afraid people in Jericho were. Everyone believed something awful was going to happen. Rahab asked the spies to safe her and her family when the Lord gave the land over to them. The men agreed.

In order to escape Rahab let the men out of her house by using a rope through the window. She was able to do this because her house was built into the city walls. Find Rahab at her window and draw in the rope. Watch out - some of the spaces lead to nowhere. One tip is to work backwards from the spy towards Rahab... you might find that easier

Her advice to the men was to hide in the hills for three days and then go back to their people. Before they left Rahab they made an agreement with her in order that she would be kept safe. They gave her a scarlet cord and told her what to do with it to make sure she and her family would be kept safe.

Cross out all the g j and p's to find out how they would be safe.

Evjerygponpe   in   tjgphje   jhogupjse   wjjilgl   bje   sjafgpe,

_ _ _ _ _ _ _ _   _ _   _ _ _   _ _ _ _ _   _ _ _ _   _ _   _ _ _ _

Igjpf   tgjphge   sjcaggrlppet   cjgpogjrd   is   tjiegpd   tgoj   tjgphjeg

_ _   _ _ _   _ _ _ _ _ _ _   _ _ _ _   _ _   _ _ _ _   _ _   _ _ _

wjignpdggogw.

_ _ _ _ _ _ .

The spies returned and told Joshua all that had happened. What happened next? Which picture do you think is the picture that really happened? Now read on to see if you were right.

Joshua and all the people went to the River Jordan and set up camp for three days. They were told that when they saw the ark of the covenant (the special box carrying the God's laws) they were to follow it, so they would know where to go. When the ark moved to the waters edge, all the people followed behind just as they had been told to. As soon as the priests carrying the ark set foot into the water the water heaped up on one side so that everyone could get through on dry land.

It was just like crossing the Red Sea all over again. The priests stood in the middle and all the people passed by on dry land.

Can you think of some things the people might have said as they reached the other side that would show how they were feeling about what had just happened?

Can you find all these words from the story so far in this wordsearch?

Joshua, Moses, covenant, water, Rahab, Jericho, walls, city, ark, scarlet, cord, king, spies, strong, courageous, obey, land promise, flax, Jordan, River, God, Canaan, rule, law.

Write down all the letters that haven't been used and put them into the spaces below. These letters are a verse from the Bible.

__ __ __ __ __ __

__ __ __ __ __

__ __ __ __ __ __

__ __ __ __ __

__ __ __ __ __

__ __ __ __ __ __

Psalm 16 Verse 1

j	o	s	h	u	a	c	k
e	s	e	k	e	r	o	e
r	p	s	i	p	k	u	m
i	i	o	n	r	e	r	s
c	e	m	g	a	c	a	c
h	s	s	a	h	i	g	a
o	f	e	w	a	t	e	r
c	o	r	d	b	y	o	l
w	a	l	l	s	o	u	e
s	t	r	o	n	g	s	t
c	o	v	e	n	a	n	t
o	b	e	y	l	a	n	d
p	r	o	m	i	s	e	g
o	u	d	f	o	n	r	c
f	l	a	x	a	i	n	a
y	e	o	d	u	i	t	n
a	k	r	i	v	e	r	a
g	o	d	e	r	e	f	a
j	u	g	e	l	a	w	n

12

The artist forgot to finish his picture. Can you complete it for him?

How many stones are there?___ The stones came from the middle of the river Jordan and were placed together as a sign to the children of the future that this was where God had stopped the water to let them pass over. It was a memorial. You can still see memorials today. Follow the oranges to find out how the kings in the lands round about were feeling.

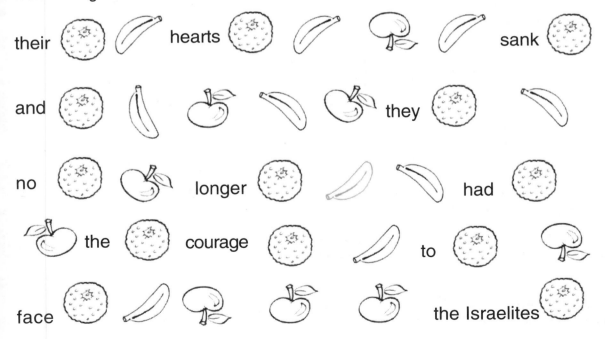

Draw expressions in the faces to show how the kings might be feeling.

The Israelites had, up to now, eaten manna, a special bread provided by God. They never starved. God always provided enough. After they had crossed the water they celebrated the Passover which was their way of remembering how God had led them out of Egypt and away from slavery. The day after the Passover there was no more manna. That was because they could now eat the produce of the land. What do you think they would eat?

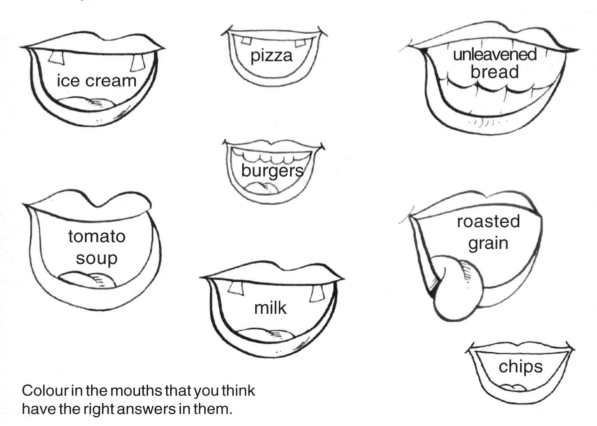

ice cream

pizza

unleavened bread

burgers

tomato soup

roasted grain

milk

chips

Colour in the mouths that you think have the right answers in them.

14

Write out your favourite menu

Starter

Main Course

Dessert

As Joshua came near to Jericho he had an amazing experience. The numbers below are coded words. Each word is separated by a dash. Use the code breaker to work out what letters replace the numbers. Place these words in order into the blank spaces in the sentence at the bottom of the page.

10 15 19 8 21 1 ▬ 19 23 15 18 4 ▬ 10 15 19 8 21 1 ▬ 23 8 15 19 5 ▬
19 9 4 5 ▬ 14 5 9 20 8 5 18 ▬ 9 ▬ 3 15 13 13 1 14 4 ▬ 1 18 13 25 ▬
12 15 18 4 ▬ 10 15 19 8 21 1 ▬ 13 5 19 19 1 7 5 ▬
3 15 13 13 1 14 4 5 18 ▬ 19 8 15 5 19 ▬ 8 15 12 25

a	b	c	d	e	f	g	h	i	j	k	l
1	2	3	4	5	6	7	8	9	10	11	12
m	n	o	p	q	r	s	t	u	v	w	x
13	14	15	16	17	18	19	20	21	22	23	24
y	z										
25	26										

_ _ _ _ _ _ looked up and saw a man with a _ _ _ _ _ _ drawn in his hand. _ _ _ _ _ _ asked

"_ _ _ _ _   _ _ _ _ are you on?

The man replied "_ _ _ _ _ _ _   _   _ _ _ _ _ _ _ the _ _ _ _ of

the _ _ _ _" _ _ _ _ _ _ fell face down. He asked

"What _ _ _ _ _ _ _ do you have?"

The _ _ _ _ _ _ _ _ _ replied "Take off your _ _ _ _ _ this is

_ _ _ _ ground.

16

Turn the page and you can see a picture of the walled city of Jericho. It was all closed up so that no-one could get in or out. The people were very afraid. The Lord gave Joshua precise instructions that had to be followed. Some words of the instructions have been missed out. Can you fill them in?

In _____ go armed men. Seven priests blowing trumpets go _____. They

are _____ by the ark of the Lord. The rear guard are at the ___ .

_____ the city once.

(front, followed, end, next circle)

Number Challenge

After doing this the people returned to the camp each night. Do the sums to find out what happens next in the story.

They did this for _____ days. $(10 + 8 \div 2 - 3)$

So the next day would be day _____. $(21 - 7 \div 2)$

This day was to be different. Everything was to be done the same but this time they were to circle the city _____ times. $(10 \times 3 \div 5 + 1)$

Unjumble the following words: So on day
VENSE _ _ _ _ _ they circled
EENSV _ _ _ _ _ times and on the
TSENHVE _ _ _ _ _ _ _ time all the people gave a loud shout. As they shouted the walls of Jericho fell down. And all the people ran forward to take the city.

How many guards can you find in the picture and how many arrows pointing out of the windows? How many windows can you spot in this picture and how many birds are flying above the city?

In this picture there are seven priests carrying the ark and there are seven priests in front blowing horns only their horns are missing. Can you find the seven missing horns? All of them are hidden somewhere in the picture.

The priests were told by God to play rams horn trumpets.
Help this priest find his trumpet.

Can you do this crossword about Joshua and Jericho?

Across

1. The main man (six letters)
6. The Israelites were journeying to the promised _ _ _ _ (four letters)
5. You have a big one on the end of your foot. _ _ _ (three letters.)
7. You need to pass a test and have a license to drive a _ _ _ (three letters)
9. The Israelites escaped from this country. (five letters)
11. There is only one true _ _ _ (three letters)
12. God has given us ten _ _ _ _ _ _ _ _ _ to obey.

Down

1. Where the walls fell down. (seven letters)
2. When you can't do it alone you need this. (four letters)
3. The opposite of Uncle. (four letters)
4. The Israelites attacked Jericho on day _ _ _ _ _. (five letters)
5. The Priests played these instruments. _ _ _ _ _ _ _ _ (eight letters)
8. The name of a sea. (three letters)
9. The opposite of West.
10. What do you do with a musical instrument? (four letters)
11. Ready, Steady _ _. (two letters)

As they ran into the city Joshua remembered Rahab. Rahab and her family were to be spared because she helped the spies. Everything else was to be destroyed. However, certain things were to be brought to God's treasury. These thins were sacred to God and were not to be kept by the people for themselves.

Joshua made sure Rahab and her family were taken to a safe place. Then everything was burnt and destroyed except for the precious things that were brought to God's house. Below you will see that there are three different kinds of containers. Take the letters in the middle of each different type of container and put them together to form three different words. This is what was gathered up and kept for God's house .

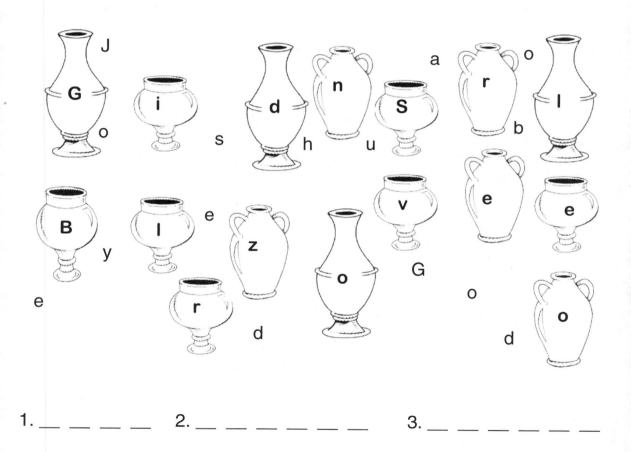

1. __ __ __ __   2. __ __ __ __ __ __   3. __ __ __ __ __ __

Joshua was well known and respected by everyone. Take the other letters that are hidden in between the vases. These will spell out why Joshua was so successful.

__ __ __ __ __ __   __ __ __ __ __ __   __ __ __

Nowadays Joshua might have been given a certificate for his work. Fill in what you think would be suitable on Joshua's certificate.

Joshua is:

Try and think up your own words to describe what Joshua was like. Write these down. What was Joshua's job? What did he do? Write this down on his certificate too. Once you have done that pick some more ideas from the words below... but remember some of these words are wrong. Which words do you think are the right ones? Circle them once you think you have found them.

Egyptian	brave	godly	obedient	nasty
cowardly	wicked	lazy	stupid	
courageous	strong	musician	soldier	
truck driver	space man	spy	commander	Israelite

Can you remember?????

These questions will test your memory. All the answers are in this book somewhere. Write your answers in the spaces provided.

1. Who led the people out of Egypt?

Moses, Joshua or Jethro

2. What did the Israelites eat in the Wilderness?

manna, crisps or fish

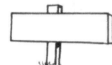

3. How many commandments did God give the Israelites?

Was it 9, 10 or 110?

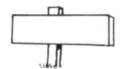

4. Where did God give Moses his commands? Was it on Mount...

5. What idol did the people make?

Was it a calf, goat or a sheep?

6. Who gave Joshua help to succeed?

Was it God, Moses or Noah?

7. Where were the people heading to?

Was it Jericho, Jethro or Jerusalem?

8. Who hid the two spies?

Was it Ruth, Rahab or Rachel?

9. What was the sign for safety?

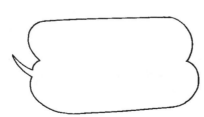

scarlet scarf, red ribbon, scarlet cord

10. What did the priests blow?

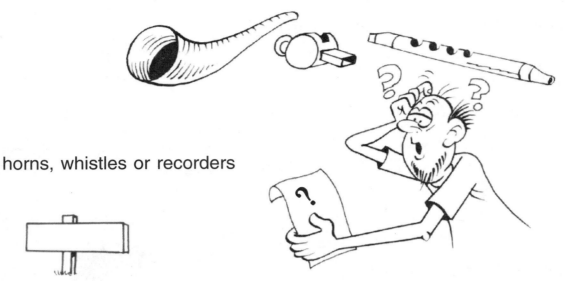

horns, whistles or recorders

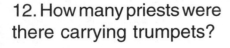

11. How many times did the Israelite army march around the city of Jericho?

7   17   3

12. How many priests were there carrying trumpets?

77   177   7

13. How many years were the Israelites travelling in the desert?

7   14   40

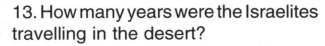

Add a brick to the wall for every correct answer. Then colour in the whole picture.

Joshua won the battle because God was with him. He went on to do great things for God. So What happened next? Follow the spiral and find out.

throughout all the land. Joshua Chapter 6 Verse 27 and his fame spread throughout all the land. Joshua Chapter 6 Verse 27 and his fame spread

So the Lord was with Joshua and his fame spread

Be very careful to love the Lord your God. Joshua Chapter 23 Verse 11

One day it came the time for Joshua to die. He gave the people one last piece of advice.
Follow the spiral round to find out what Joshua said. It is a good piece of advice for you too.

28

ANSWERS

p2 Games, life, football, school, traffic; There would be chaos.

p3
1. Worship no other gods but me.
2. Do not bow down to any other god and worship it.
3. Do not use God's name in a wrong way.
4. Keep Sunday holy.
5. Respect your Father and your Mother.
6. Do not kill.
7. Do not commit adultery.
8. Do not steal.
9. Do not tell lies.
10. Do not want things that other people have.

p5 It has good food; there are huge cities; we can defeat them; they have strong walls; the people are big and strong.

p6 As I was with Moses so I will be with you.
Be strong and courageous and obey my law.

p8 Bring out the men who came to you. They are spies.

p10 Everyone in the house will be safe if the scarlet cord is tied to the window.
Picture 3.

p11 Thank you God, Hurray, Amazing, God is so great, I am dry,
It is a miracle, I am so happy.

p13. 12 Stones
Their hearts sank and they no longer had the courage to face the Israelites.

p 14. unleavened bread, roasted grain, milk.

p 16. Joshua looked up and saw a man with a sword drawn in his hand. Joshua asked "'Whose side are you on?" The man replied "Neither, I command the army of the Lord." Joshua fell face down. He asked "What message do you have?" The commander replied "Take off your shoes this is holy ground."

p17. In front go armed men. Seven priests blowing trumpets go next. They are followed by the ark of the Lord. The rear guard are at the end. Circle the city once.
6 days; seven; seven.   Seven; Seven; Seventh.

p 18. nine guards; four arrows; eight windows; five birds.
The trumpets are hidden: two on the city walls; two in the ark of the covenant; two in the aprons of two of the priests and one on the ground by Joshua's feet.

p 20. Across. 1. Joshua; 5. Toe; 6. Land; 7. Car; 9. Egypt; 11. God; 12. Commands.
Down. 1. Jericho; 2. Help; 3. Aunt; 4. Seven; 5. Trumpets; 8. Red; 9. East; 10. Play; 11. Go.

j	o	s	h	u	a	c	k
e	s	e	k	e	r	o	e
r	p	s	i	p	k	u	m
i	i	o	n	r	e	r	s
c	e	m	g	a	c	a	c
h	s	s	a	h	i	g	a
o	f	e	w	a	t	e	r
c	o	r	d	b	y	o	l
w	a	l	l	s	o	u	e
s	t	r	o	n	g	s	t
c	o	v	e	n	a	n	t
o	b	e	y	l	a	n	d
p	r	o	m	i	s	e	g
o	u	d	f	o	n	r	c
f	l	a	x	a	i	n	a
y	e	o	d	u	i	t	n
a	k	r	i	v	e	r	a
g	o	d	e	r	e	f	a
j	u	g	e	l	a	w	n

p 12. Word search solution.

Keep me safe O God for in you I take refuge.
Psalm 16 Verse 1.

p 21. Gold; Silver; Bronze.
p 21 Joshua obeyed God.
p 22 brave; godly; obedient; courageous; strong; a soldier; spy; commander; Israelite.
p 23-26 Moses; Manna; 10; Sinai; a calf; God; Jericho; Rahab;
Scarlet cord; horns; 7; 7; 40.
p 28 So the Lord was with Joshua and his fame spread throughout all the land.
Joshua Chapter 6 Verse 27.
Be very careful to love the Lord your God. Joshua Chapter 23 Verse 11.

1. Worship no other gods but me. This command means that we should not put anyone or anything before God. He should be the most important person in our life.

2. Do not bow down to any other god and worship it. This command means that we should not worship or give our love to any other god. The God of the Bible is the only true God that there is. All other gods are false.

3. Do not use God's name in a wrong way. This command means that we should not use God's name as a swear word or use his name in anger. Some people when they are angry shout out God's name or Jesus' name in a horrible way. We should only speak about God in a loving and respectful way.

4. Keep Sunday holy. This is God's special day. We should remember to spend some special time with God worshipping him and praising him. We should always spend time with God but we should make sure that we spend extra time with him on Sunday. This is God's special day for us to rest from all normal work and to focus on him.

5. Respect your Father and your Mother. This command means that we should obey our parents. We shouldn't be nasty to them and disobey them. We should be loving and helpful to them. Thank God for your parents or for the people who love and look after you.

6. Do not kill. Killing people is wrong. Hurting them and fighting with them is wrong too. We should love other people. We should treat them just as we would like to be treated.

7. Do not commit adultery. This is a command for grown-ups. It means that when men and women get married they should stay married. When they marry they promise each other to love each other always. Adultery is another word for when people break this promise. We should always keep our promises.

8. Do not steal. This command means that it is wrong to take something that does not belong to you. So do not take people's toys or sweets without their permission.

9. Do not tell lies. This command means that it is wrong to say something that is not true.

10. Do not want things that other people have. This command means that it is wrong to be greedy and to want more and more things. God is good to us. He gives us lots of good things. We should thank him for what he gives us and be content.

Look out for the series: God's Little Guide books published by Christian Focus. These are all about the ten commandments and how two children called Sam and Katy find out how to obey God's commands.

Love me (ISBN 185792 3510)
God's special Name (185792-3537)
Love Mum and Dad (ISBN: 185792-3553)
A special promise (ISBN:185792-357X)
Tell The Truth (ISBN: 185792-3596)

Too Many Toys (ISBN: 185792-3529)
God's special day (ISBN: 185792-3545)
Love others (ISBN:185792-3561)
This belongs to (ISBN: 185792-3588)
Thanks God (185792-360X)

Text by Ruth Maclean Illustrations by Barrie Appleby
© Christian Focus Publications 1999
Printed in Great Britain by JW Arrowsmith ISBN 1 85792 473 8
Published by Christian Focus Publications Geanies House, Fearn, Tain, Ross-shire, IV20 1TW, Scotland
www.christianfocus.com

Do you like puzzles? Have you enjoyed this book? Here are further puzzles for you to enjoy...

The beautiful bride - Rebecca ISBN 1 85792 1399

The Brave Ruler - Daniel ISBN 1 85792 0880

God's Builder - Nehemiah ISBN 1 85792 0538

The Great Celebration - Hezekiah ISBN 1 85792 1380

The Happy Harvest - Ruth ISBN 1 85792 2468

The Man who Ran - Jonah ISBN 1 85792 228X

The Queen's Feast - Esther ISBN 1 85792 0899

The Wise King - Solomon ISBN 1 85792 052X

The Shepherd King - David ISBN 1 85792 3030

The Desert Leader - Moses ISBN 1 85792 3049

The Big Contest - Elijah ISBN 1 85792 472X

Published by Christian Focus Publications
Geanies House, Fearn, Tain, Ross-shire, IV20 1TW, Scotland
www.christianfocus.com